Classical Education

&

The Homeschool

Douglas Wilson
Wes Callihan
Douglas Jones

Douglas Wilson, Wesley Callihan, and Douglas Jones,
Classical Education and the Home School (revised version)

© 2001 by Canon Press,
P.O. Box 8729, Moscow, ID 83843
1-800-488-2034
www.canonpress.org

ISBN: 1-885767-85-4

Contents

Introduction

As we survey the educational ruins around us, classical and Christian education appears to be an idea whose time has come. Actually, in the light of history, it is a concept whose time has come *again*. More and more Christian parents are seeing the failures of modern socialistic education—and these failures have been monumental—such parents are hungering for a *substantive* alternative, one that has been tested before, and found to be good. Classical and Christian education presents them with just such an alternative.

Parents are coming to see that it is simply not enough to pull the kids out of the government schools. When a demon is cast out, and nothing put in its place, the final result can be seven times worse (Mt. 12:45). Reactionary Christian education is consequently not really a permanent alternative. Many Christian parents who had initially just reacted to the godlessness of the government schools are now seeing the shallowness of that kind of Christian response. They have become hungry, on behalf of their children, for an education that is unabashedly Christian, rigorous, and thorough. At the same time, parents who think this way also commonly acknowledge they really do not fully understand what it is they desire.

This brief treatment aims to present some of the basic principles and methods of a classical and Christian education, tailored for use in a homeschool setting. One of the primary purposes of classical education is to equip the students to learn for themselves. So, in a similar way, the purpose of this booklet is to set interested parents on this path and to give them some of the basic information they will need to walk on it. Even though it is an unfamiliar path to many of us, it is still well-worn from centuries of use, and it should be possible for us to feel at home there once again.

At the same time, we should remember that a classical and Christian education is not a "package deal." No one supplier or textbook publisher will provide you with everything you need in a fifty-pound box, delivered by UPS. Western culture weighs more than this, and the abandonment of the fast-food, convenience-store mentality which currently surrounds education is one of the first indications that we are making significant progress.

In a very real sense, this kind of classical education results in a certain mindset, a certain orientation. It is that mindset which is briefly set forth and commended in this small booklet. Parents who undertake this pattern for education will, of necessity, feel very alone in some respects. But as the process continues, they will make many friends—some living and walking the same path with them, and many others dead and pleasantly entombed in their favorite books.

So what is presented here is nothing more than amiable company for the first few steps on these "older paths" and a rough, sketched-out map for the remainder of the journey. *Deus vobiscum.*

The Necessity for Hard Work

To give to someone else what one never received one's self is, of course, difficult. Many parents are initially attracted to the idea of a classical education because they know that they were shortchanged in their own education; they want their children to be taught in a way that they were not. The problem with this is a problem common in all forms of conversion, including academic conversions—one is turning away from the familiar to embrace the unfamiliar. The word conversion comes from the Latin *converto*, which means "I turn around." Turning around, turning away from the familiar to the unfamiliar can be rather unnerving at times.

One may be disquieted by what passes for education today without really understanding what education ought to be. Coming to that fuller understanding is a *process*, and in the early stages of that process thinking parents will feel as though their efforts are little more than a farce. Your friends may be asking, "Who do you think you are?" If they are polite enough not to ask in a loud voice, you may still be supplying the question on their behalf.

The only way to answer such questions successfully is through a commitment to hard work over a long period of time. We are tempted to think it would be nice if education could occur on the Big Rock Candy Mountain. But it cannot, and as diligent parents, we are confronted with two areas which stand out with respect to the necessity of hard work.

The first is the necessity of reading, and reading some more. A person can successfully sell someone else on a vacuum cleaner without reading, but he cannot sell someone else on books without reading. *Education is the process of selling someone on books.* Parents who will not read simply cannot be equipped to supply a classical and Christian education for their children. Tragically, even many Christians have been infected with the "affirmative action" approach to learning. We want equal results for unequal effort, but God did not create the world in this way. He is not mocked; unequal efforts will routinely bring us unequal results. This means that we cannot pursue a classical and Christian education as a fad; we are not purchasing intellectual hula hoops for the kids.

While the volume of reading is important, the quality of books read is far more important. Because of this, we conclude many of the sections of this booklet with a suggested reading list for parents. The books suggested will not all be "about" education, but they will all be directly connected to the task of bringing this kind of education to your children. And as you read these books, they will in turn suggest further reading. These lists included here are intended to mark the starting blocks, not the finish line.

The reason we recommend a particular book may not be immediately obvious, and many Christian parents may wonder if some are even worth reading. But for those who undertake the task, the reasons will soon become obvious. Again, the lists are not exhaustive but only a good beginning.

Diligent reading is related to the *second* area where hard work is necessary—that is, in the area of instruction. Children need to be *taught*. Occasionally, a self-motivated and bright child will show the ability to become an *autodidact*—*i.e.* self-taught. But most children need to be led into an understanding of what they are being taught. The ability to learn on one's own is normally the *result* of a good education, and not normally the *cause* of it. Jesus teaches us that a "disciple is not above his teacher, nor a servant above his master" (Mt. 10:24).

This means that there must be consistent time set aside for instruction in the home, and the parental instructors must be *prepared* to provide that instruction. The reading mentioned above is a significant part of that preparation. Glibness, or an ability to "wing it" is no substitute for reading and study. And while it may be possible to "wow" the younger children, there will come a time when your older children will detect the fraud if you are not prepared. For example, in the area of literature, the students may read and enjoy books that their parents have not read, but they cannot be *taught* literature that their parents have not read. More than this, they cannot be taught literature that their parents have not *studied*.

The last important note is certainly not last in order of importance. The Bible teaches that doctrine—teaching—must be *adorned*. If it is not adorned with a gracious manner and clean-hearted living, the child will likely either come to imitate the hypocrisy of the parents or turn away with disgust from everything given to him, including what was truly valuable. Neither direction is one we should want our children to take. Consequently, the rigor of classical study must not be confused with the rigors of living in an unpleasant home. Consider exhortation from a father in a former century:

> [A child's] character is forming under a principle, not of choice, but of nurture. The spirit of the house is breathed into his nature, day by day. The anger and gentleness, the fretfulness and patience—the appetites, passions, and manners—all the variant moods of feeling exhibited round him, pass into him as impressions, and become seeds of character in him; not because the parents will, but because

it must be so, whether they will or not. They propagate their own evil in the child, not by design, but under a law of moral infection. . . . The spirit of the house is in the members of the children by nurture, not by teaching, not by any attempt to communicate the same, but because it is the air the children breathe. . . . Understand that it is the family spirit, the organic life of the house, the silent power of a domestic godliness, working as it does, unconsciously and with sovereign effect—this it is which forms your children to God.[1]

A Brief Description of
Classical and Christian Education

Classical education can best be understood as referring
to three rudimentary things. The first has to do with
educational method, that is, the pattern of conducting
the student through the stages of *grammar*, *dialectic*, and
rhetoric. Collectively, these three stages have been called
the *trivium*. Although methods of education are not all-
important, as some modern pedagogues have assumed,
methodology still retains some degree of importance.

The second aspect of classical learning refers to the
content of the studies, and answers the question, "What
subjects are to be studied?" Classical education is dis-
tinguished by the presence of subjects like Latin, logic,
theology, and rhetoric in the curriculum. At the same
time, many of the subjects common to a basic education are also included—history, science, mathematics,
etc., omitting classes on Getting In Touch With One's
Own Personal Self.

The third aspect recognizes the importance of the
historical and cultural position of the teacher and student. Classical and Christian education is indigenous
to Western culture; it is the result of Christ being born
during the reign of Caesar Augustus and of the earliest
missionaries heading west more than they did east or
south. Christian parents who seek to impart this heri-
tage to their children are not being xenophobic, or hos-
tile to other cultures. As Christianity permeates the Far
East, for example, its cultural impact will certainly be
glorious—and quite different from what we have seen
in the history of our civilization. But we do not honor
another culture by disparaging the achievements of our
own culture. Parents who give their children a classical
and Christian education are simply recognizing that, in
the providence of God, their children have been born

into Western culture; the only choice remaining is whether they will be educated poorly or well.

Other Senses of *Classical*

Apart from the preceding sense of *classical*, you'll find two other uses of the term in the realm of education. For different reasons, evangelical Christians ought to reject both. With regard to the first, the reason for this is obvious. For some, *classical* means neo-pagan. In the Renaissance, many wanted to return to the paganism of ancient Athens and Rome. But we know from Scripture that the rock of Daniel's vision has struck that particular statue on its feet and destroyed it, and it can never be restored. As Christians we should not *want* it restored, and as creatures, we must be careful not to fight against the decrees of Providence. God destroyed those civilizations, and our duty is to say "Amen" and "Good riddance." We may study the remnants of those cultures with pleasure and profit, but not from any misguided desire to return to those rebellious cultures from which God delivered us. As Dorothy Sayers pointed out, "Our civilization, such as it is, remains in its living bones a Christian civilization—and the Augustan Latin was never Christian."

Another approach to classical education may be more problematic for some Protestant Christians. This is seen in the rigorous classical study remaining today in some parts of the Roman Catholic church. Of course, the study of Latin is kept alive there, as well as a self-conscious historical and cultural connection with the medieval world. Thomas Aquinas and others brought the ancient philosophy of Aristotle into the modern world, trying to merge it with a Christian worldview. We would go too far afield to address in detail here the reasons for rejecting such an approach, but not least of them is the inseparable connection between Catholic theology, which is certainly unbiblical, and Thomism. Another reason concerns the autonomous use of natural law by Aquinas. In short, the classical Protestant should not be seeking a return to the theology of the medieval scholastics.

Education in Early America

When we speak of a classical education, we speak not only of ancient and medieval visions but also of that education common to older Britain and transplanted into early America. The classical English emphasis on a mastery of language disciplines, especially Latin and rhetoric, helped ground generations of superior leaders and thinkers.

Traditionally, a classical education began either in the home or a local grammar school, and, for some, continued through into its depths in the college years. That great Puritan thinker Cotton Mather summarized early Harvard's basic requirements for incoming students. Notice the striking contrast of expectations between the grammar schools of yesteryear and those of our own day:

> When scholars had so far profited at the *grammar schools*, that they could read any *classical author* into English, and readily make and speak true *Latin*, and write it in *verse* as well as *prose*; and perfectly decline the *paradigms* of *nouns* and *verbs* in the Greek tongue, they were judged capable of admission in *Harvard College*.[2]

Similarly, early Yale required,

> That none may expect to be admitted into this College unless upon examination of the

President and Tutors, they shall be found able
extempore to read, construe, and parce Tully,
Virgil, and the Greek Testament: and to write
true Latin prose and to understand the Rules
of Prosodia, and common arithmetic, and
shall bring sufficient testimony of his blame-
less and inoffensive life.[3]

Most other colleges expected similar classical training
as the basis for a student *starting* work in higher education. But these early schools expected not just profi-
ciency in languages, they also expected students to study
within an explicitly Christian framework to the glory
of God. For the devout, a *secular classical* education was
a contradiction in terms. Take for example the stated
purposes of early William and Mary College of 1727.
Note below how the statement naturally combines classical and Christian (Protestant) aspects in its purposes:

Toward the cultivating the minds of men, and
rectifying their manners, what a mighty in-
fluence the studies of good letters, and the
liberal sciences have, appears from hence, that
these studies not only flourished of old
amongst those famous nations, the Hebrews,
Egyptians, Greeks, and Romans; but in the
latter ages of the world likewise, after a great
interruption and almost destruction of them,
through the incursions of the barbarous nations, they are at last retrieved, and set up with
honor in all considerable nations. Upon this
there followed the reformation of many errors and abuses in the point of religion, and
the institution of youth to the duties of Christian virtues and civility; and a due preparation of fit persons for all offices in church
and state.[4]

The early Harvard statutes similarly declare that "everyone shall consider the main end of his life and studies, to know God and Jesus Christ which is Eternal life—Jn. 17.3."[5] Obviously, these early colleges have long since betrayed their original purposes in regard to both classical and Christian education. Nonetheless, in their godly prime, they left us many influential Christian leaders, thinkers, and citizens.

This, however, brings a basic question to the front. What *is* meant by a Christian worldview and a Christian education? Christian education is *not* a secular and humanistic education with prayer and Bible class attached to it. Rather, we view the Scriptures as the sole rule of faith and practice. The Bible must be at the center of our thinking. It is not central as a vase of flowers is central to a table—nice, but decorative only—but rather central as an axle is central. Everything in the educational process is to revolve around the revealed Word of God. The Bible, and the Bible alone, occupies this position. As the Reformers put it, in Latin, the language of the Reformation, *tota et sola Scriptura*. Our final allegiance is to *all* of Scripture, and *only* Scripture.

Component Parts of a
Classical and Christian Education

The three stages of the *trivium* are *grammar, dialectic* (or logic), and *rhetoric*. In medieval education they supplied the structure for one's general education before proceeding on to what was called the *quadrivium*.

In the grammar stage, the student learns many particulars, many facts. Note that the word *grammar* here is *not* restricted to language study. Each area of study has a "grammar." The particulars in each subject are many and various. In math, grammar would include division and multiplication tables. In geography, it would include continents, rivers, mountains, and so on. In history, it would include kings, battles, wars, dates, etc. In Latin, it includes case endings, verb endings, and basic vocabulary.

Then follows the dialectic stage, where the student begins examining the relationship between these particulars. What is the relationship between the geography of the East Coast and the first battle of Bull Run? Between Xerxes and Esther? Or, for that matter, between Genesis and the theory of evolution? The student learns about the inter-relatedness of the various subjects he has been learning up this point.

Once the student has learned the basic rudiments, and he has sorted them into piles, the student then learns to express these aquisitions in a more polished way. This is the study of rhetoric.

Now as Dorothy Sayers points out in her seminal essay, "The Lost Tools of Learning," these three aspects of the *trivium* correspond nicely to three stages of child development. She argues in that essay that our responsibility in education is to "cut with the grain," and require specific things of the students when they are most receptive to them.

She divides children into three groups. The first group is the youngest, and is characterized by her as the "Poll-parrot" stage. This corresponds generally to younger children, ages five through ten. At this age, children love to chant and memorize, and it is simply foolish not to take full advantage of the opportunity. It is just as agreeable for them to chant *amo, amas, amat* as it is for them to recite *hickory, dickory, dock*. The mastery of the grammar stage requires large amounts of memorization, and Sayers argues that this should be done when memorization is easy and agreeable. Consequently, with the classical approach, the younger children are brought to store away in memory large amounts of information which they do not yet understand. *That* comes at the next stage. Therefore, they memorize presidents, case endings, math tables, spelling words, rivers, and on and on, *ad infinitum*.

The next stage she calls the "Pert" stage. During the junior-high years, children become inquisitive, and they begin to challenge much of what they have been taught, seeking to understand it. There are two errors made at this stage. The first is made by relativistic parents, who let their child question in an open-ended fashion, and who permit the child to question in an autonomous, disrespectful way. But the second mistake is commonly made by Christian parents who feel threatened if a child questions *any* of what he has been taught; they sometimes mistakenly assume that all such questioning must be rebellious.

This pert stage is a golden opportunity to teach the student the laws of logic and proper argumentation. When the child wants to argue, he should be taught proper and responsible argumentation. The study of formal logic should begin at this age (eleven to thirteen), and the application of it *to all other subjects* should be actively encouraged. At the same time, respect for parental authority must be maintained. Children should not be permitted under any circumstances to pop off. "But Mom, that's the naturalistic fallacy!" There is no better opportunity to teach respect for others than by requiring a diligent and careful analysis of their statements and arguments.

The third stage is the rhetorical stage. In the high-school years, children become more concerned with appearances, and they should be taught how to present themselves well, communicating what they believe in a worthy fashion.

Theology is not excluded from this process. As the queen of the sciences, the Christian worldview is central. For example, in the grammar stage, children memorize verses, books, and basic doctrines of the Bible. In the dialectic stage they learn to think through various problems in the light the Word supplies—"Was it right for the Hebrew midwives to lie to Pharaoh?" In the rhetorical stage, they learn to take what they have learned and present a thoughtful presentation and apology for the Christian faith.

This is a broad outline of the education we have in mind. To fill in this content, we turn to brief excursions into language, imagination, Latin, logic, rhetoric, and worldview, as some of the more unique aspects of classical education. It's very easy to talk about any education as if it were purely a disembodied, intellectual endeavor. But Christianity loves the body and creation, and central to that vision is an exercised imagination. We turn to that aspect of content first.

The Glory of Language and Imagination.
Language has always sat at the heart of classical education, and yet language is rather bizarre. Babies can use it, and yet it involves mysteries which even the most

profound scholars haven't untied. It looks so simple, but it can turn the world inside out.

We're so used to language that we can pass over it with a yawn, especially in education. We tend to think that language is just another handy tool, like a multiplication table or a pen. But language pulls together so many parts of life in powerful ways. It is far more than a simple tool. And Scripture puts language right at the center of so much.

God created the world by speaking. The Fall came through false speech. The Law came in "ten words." Redemption came through the Word made flesh. The Holy Spirit was poured out through the tongues of many nations. And in the end, we will be judged "by every idle word" we speak.

What is it about language that makes it so central? Perhaps we get some hint of this from the Incarnation itself. In the Incarnation, the invisible was made visible. The second person of the Godhead took on flesh and bone. Something like this happens every time we speak or write. The invisible world of our personality takes on physical features, whether through these material squiggles of ink or voice sounds. In every case, hidden things are revealed.

But something more is going on too. It's not just a revealing of the invisible, as mysterious as that is. It's change too. The world changes. When God spoke the creation exploded into existence. When the Word took on flesh, history was reversed. The invisible redirected the visible in new ways. In both of these cases, the "subjunctive"—that which could be—shaped the "what is." Divine imagination redraws things within language and then changes them in the material world—He "calls those things which do not exist as though they did" (Rom. 4:17).

As creatures, we can create change in a similar way. Imagination-through-language gets us to picture a different world from that which surrounds us. This imaginary world often turns things around, so we can see more clearly where change is needed. One of the best Scriptural examples of this is Nathan's rebuke of David. In order to have Bathsheba, David set her husband up to be killed. When God sent Nathan the prophet to rebuke David, the Lord had him tell David a story about a poor man and his lamb. In other words, God had Nathan use an imaginary world of language to change the actual world. David was enraged by the injustice in Nathan's "world." Imagination was able to reorder the world and break through a wall of sin.

But it even goes deeper than this. It's not just that we can depict imaginary worlds by means of language. Even the most ordinary pieces of language demand imagination. For example, we speak of personal difficulties as if they were actual heavy things (burdens) and goals as if they were targets ("I'm hunting for a job"). We speak of beauty as a physical force ("She knocked me out") and the mind as a machine ("I'm a little rusty"). In Scripture, grace produces "fruit," faith is a "substance," and Christ is a "lion." In all these cases, we are imagining one thing in the shadow of something else; we are renaming one bit of creation in light of another. This happens almost all the time in everyday speech, but it's so common we tend to only notice the flashy acts of language found in stories or poems.

Language, then, not only reveals the invisible, it allows us to rename the world and change it. Of course, one can rename faithfully ("Christ is a lamb") or rebelliously ("Christ is a mosquito"). Not all naming produces the right kind of change. Much of it can mislead us and allow non-Christian imaginations to dictate Christian living. That's why we have to watch our language and examine the images we so commonly invoke in the midst of Christian living.

But if we try to speak and name faithfully, then language can help us transform the world for the better. When God renamed various saints in Scripture, he was starting them on a new course, a new creation. Properly identifying compassion, justice, tyranny, and celebration in contrast to popular lies brings the Christian imagination into contact with the real world. Our language helps redirect our imaginations, and our imaginations redirect the world by God's hand.

More positively, we use language not only to change the bad but to create the beautiful. All the arts begin with imagination and language. And they allow us to see things in other ways, in creative ways. They redraw the world and can wake us out of our laziness. They can remind us to love the beautiful and despise the evil. Similarly, our laughter comes from using our language-led imaginations to line up the world in odd ways that don't fit. Our laughter says "no, that's not the way it's supposed to go." Creativity, delight, and laughter all involve imagining one part of the world in terms of another.

But all of these parts of our sanctification—storytelling, ruling, creating, delighting—require that we pay attention to the language arts. Whether we are opening up other worlds through foreign or ancient languages or learning to write poetry or modeling creation imaginatively for the sciences, we have to be intimately familiar with the subtleties and images that permeate our language. We have to master the basics of grammar and vocabulary and figurative language before we can effectively reflect God's creative use of language. Any education that minimizes language and imagination is desperately seeking failure. Classical and Christian education delights in it.

Imagination and Fiction

Language and imagination come through most powerfully in fiction. We should be pierced through when we
hear Christian parents glibly proclaiming that they don't
want their children to hear fairy tales or fiction of any
sort. It sounds like a certain death sentence. It sounds
like the parent is saying, "I'm really hoping to raise im
beciles and perverts to the glory of God."

A well-exercised imagination is crucial to making
moral and rational judgments. Both ethics and logic assume imagination as a starting point. Those who lack a
dynamic imagination will never be able to grow into
mature wisdom. They will always be stuck in very nar-
row, self-centered mental grooves, following infantile
rules.

In the case of morality, many thinkers have pointed
to the fact that moral judgments involve the imaginative act of placing yourself in the other person's place,
the act of sympathy. Even the simplest, yet most profound commands—"You shall love your neighbor as
yourself" (Mt. 22:39) and "love one another as I have
loved you" (Jn. 15:12)—require us to imagine one person as another, one situation in terms of another, Christ
as us. That involves a profound and imaginative metaphorical transfer. And that has to be learned; the impli-
cations are very subtle.

Similarly, when we pray "forgive us our debts, as
we forgive our debtors" (Mt. 6:12), we (terrifyingly)
invoke one imagined reality and ask it to be applied to
us. Interpersonally, we are commanded to imagine and
treat others "in lowliness of mind let each esteem other
better than themselves" (Phil. 2:3).

Not only love, but faith and hope, too, involve a
very creative imagination. Faith, of course, "is the substance of things hoped for, the evidence of things not

seen" (Heb. 11:1). More concretely, Abraham "against hope believed in hope, that he might become the father of many nations" (Rom. 4:18). This gets explained in terms of Abraham's imagination: "accounting that God was able to raise [Isaac] up, even from the dead" (Heb. 11:19).

Now where are we supposed to learn how to project these very intricate patterns and schemes of imagination required in faith, hope, and love? Are we really supposed to believe that we can starve our childrens' imaginations for twenty years and then magically expect them to have any ability at all to imitate Christ or Abraham? That's like making a child sit still for his whole childhood so that he can sprint in the Olympics when he's twenty. Rubber legs won't cut it. And it will be far too late to start. The same goes for imagination.

But it's not only moral judgments that suffer from a defective imagination. Plain reasoning does too. One of the common myths about logic is that it can free us from that "nasty" world of metaphor and imagination. Almost every logic text goes to some pains to explain why metaphor has to be reduced or exiled from logical discourse. Logic can't handle figurative language, so it has to be reduced to the literal. As one classic mathematical logic text explains: "Use of formal languages will allow us to escape from the imprecision and ambiguities of natural languages"[6]

The irony is, of course, that logic itself grows out of some very basic metaphors that quickly get forgotten. Peruse a logic text sometime in search of the various root metaphors that do so much real grunt work in logic. Take, for example, the popular college-level text by Bergmann, where "argument" is defined in terms of something like a pancake stack: "An argument is a set of sentences one of which (the conclusion) is taken to be supported by the remaining sentences (the premises)."[7]

But propositions or sentences aren't really bricks or pancakes, but that sort of metaphorical mapping of concrete objects onto abstract logic doesn't end at introductory definitions. The nature of logical inference itself is regularly defined in terms of a metaphorical path of some sort. Sainsbury and countless others explain that "one way in which premises can give good reason for a conclusion is for the conclusion to follow from the premises"[8] But premises can't literally "follow" anything like an elephant or a river do. When Sainsbury starts to explain "following" he continues metaphorically: "The logician wants to say that [arguments] are valid in virtue of their pattern or form, the same in each case."[9] And so inference now is thought of in terms of molds of some sort, rarely if ever specified any further.

All of morality and reasoning involve imagination and metaphor. They can't get off the ground without it. And we learn to exercise our imaginations in stories— fiction and fantasy and fairy tales most tellingly. But far deeper than either morality or logic is the importance of a sense of *play* for all of life. It is a joy and fascination with creation and life that imagination fosters most of all. That drives everything else, including the parental part of what our children turn out to be.

Classical and Christian home education ought to be swimming in language and imagination. Families often have even greater opportunities for this sort of endeavor than institutional schools. It is within this context of imagination and wonder, though, that all the traditional disciplines of history, mathematics, geography, etc. find their home. Of particular note for classical education are the disciplines of Latin, logic, and rhetoric. To these we now turn.

The Basics of Latin

Many reasons commend the study of Latin; we supply just a few of the more basic reasons here.

First, the study of Latin provides an efficient way to learn the grammatical structure of English. As Sayers comments, "English is a highly sophisticated, highly analytical language, whose forms, syntax and construction can be grasped and handled correctly only by a good deal of hard reasoning. . . . To embark on any complex English construction without the Latin Grammar is like trying to find one's way across country without map or signposts."

Second, Latin is a key to about fifty percent of our English vocabulary. Whether such words come to us directly from Latin, or via the Romance languages, many of our words have a Latin source. Understanding the Latin provides the student with many opportunities to enhance his English vocabulary.

In the third place, Latin is the key to all the Romance languages (which are simply great-grandchildren of Latin), and it is indirectly a key to all inflected languages. These Romance languages include Portuguese, Spanish, French, Italian, *etc.* The study of Latin will greatly help the student who goes on to study *any* of these other languages. Latin is a much greater help in the study of Spanish than, say, French is a help in the study of Spanish.

Fourth, the precision of mind required in the study of Latin is a great benefit in other fields requiring such precision—science, for example. The study of Latin requires an attention to detail which, if it has become habitual, can only be a great blessing in other subjects.

Fifth, the literature of western culture is saturated with Latin. As Sayers mentions, "without some knowledge of Latin it must be very difficult to make anything of it." History, philosophy, law, and literature all require some acquaintance with the Latin language. In many Christian homeschooling families, the question of Greek study may arise. The study of Greek certainly is valuable, but, other things being equal, it is still our conviction that Latin should take priority. But other things are not always equal. Greek, however, may still win out in the minds of some. Many families want their children to be able to study the New Testament in the original, and far more Christian parents have already studied Greek than Latin. Moreover, because of the connection to the New Testament, far more reference helps are available for Greek. At the same time, Greek *will* remain a harder language for your children to master. But for those parents who are committed to Greek, we would commend the study of Latin as a good platform for the *subsequent* study of Greek. In our own studies, Greek came first, and it would have been easier had it been the other way around.

The Basics of Teaching Latin Pronunciation

Numerous texts and programs are available to aid the homeschooling parent in teaching Latin to the kids. Nearly all of them have some instruction near the beginning concerning the proper pronunciation of Latin, but nearly all are equally unsuccessful in convincing those parents that their pronunciation is adequate. Consequently, some background is in order.

First, you are not teaching *conversational* Latin. Unlike Spanish or French or other modern languages, no culture today speaks Latin. For some this is an argument against teaching Latin at all, and if the purpose of language study were only to aid one in conversations with native speakers, the point would be a good one. But the value of Latin is not found in repartee with ancient Romans. Because this is the case, pronunciation is not nearly as important as it is with modern language study. Mispronouncing Spanish will get you laughed at in Mexico City; the same is not true of "mispronouncing" Latin.

Second, because microphones were not thrust in Augustus Caesar's face, with all his pronouncements duly recorded on tape, we are not exactly sure what his pronunciation was. The educated guesses of classical scholars will show up in texts which follow the "classical" method of pronunciation. This is the school which pronounces *v's* as *w's*, *c's* as always hard like *k*, *etc.* Still, more than a few are not entirely convinced that Latin was really pronounced that way. And, even assuming this pronunciation has been accurately reconstructed, we must recall that it was the pronunciation of the intelligentsia during the brief moments of Augustan glory. We have no transcendent reason why we must endure tremendous turmoil for the sake of maintaining this particular pattern of pronunciation.

This is related to the third point. There are alternative approaches to Latin pronunciation. One approach is the ecclesiastical pronunciation. Some Latin dictionaries will list an ecclesiastical pronunciation key in the front alongside the classical, or antiquarian, pronunciation. The ecclesiastical pronunciation is that used today in the Roman Catholic church, as well as in old Latin hymns, *etc.*

But the third method, simplest of all, is called the "Protestant," "Old," or "English" method. It follows the bright idea of linking Latin pronunciation to the vernacular. In other words, say it as though it were English.

In all of this, the one thing which is really important about pronunciation is simple consistency, so that a young student is not bewildered or confused. "But I thought you said . . ." In other respects, pronunciation *non est tanti.* It is no big deal. This may upset some classical "purists," but as Dorothy Sayers argued, "The great reproach cast up against Latin by those who would drive it altogether from the schools is that it is a dead language. But if it is dead today, it is because the Classical Scholars killed it by smothering it with too much love." The greatest value of Latin for most students is indirect, and pronunciation is not really related to such indirect benefits. And for those students who stay with their Latin, most of them will encounter most of it on the printed page. So parents should not worry about it, and, as Sayers advises, "Choose a pronunciation and stick to it."

The Basics of Teaching Latin Grammar

What is said here is presented as a very brief introduction to a few elements of Latin grammar. It may serve the purpose of removing any fear caused by the detailed but intimidating explanations found in the Latin grammars.

The grammatical function of words in English is determined largely by word order. This is not the case for Latin, which is an inflected language. To illustrate, if the words in an English sentence were moved around, "out of order," the result is a complete change in the meaning of the sentence. For example:

> *The boy hit the ball.*
> *The ball hit the boy.*

Here we have the same words, and two completely different concepts. We can take it even further into the realm of nonsense.

> *The the boy ball hit.*

But in Latin, the function of words is determined by the ending placed on the word. For example, the

ending -*am* means that a noun is the direct object of the
sentence. The ending -*a* means it is the subject, and so
forth. Thus:

> *Puella poetam amat.*
> > The girl loves the poet.
> *Poetam puella amat.*
> > The girl loves the poet.
> *Amat poetam puella.*
> > The girl loves the poet.
> *Amat puella poetam.*
> > The girl loves the poet.

In order to say that the poet loves the girl we would
have to change the endings and say:

> *Poeta puellam amat.*

When young children are memorizing their case
endings, they are simply memorizing the various endings that can be placed on the end of a noun—ten for
each noun, five singular and five plural. One set of endings is called the First Declension (there are only five
declensions) and goes *a, ae, ae, am, a, ae, arum, is, as, is.*

The same sort of thing happens with the verbs, with
different endings signaling what person, number, tense,
voice, and mood the verb is in. For example, the endings for the present tense, active voice are *o, s, t, mus,
tis, nt.* Thus, *amo* means "I love," *amas* means "you love,"
and *amat* means "he, she, or it loves." Simple, and as my
old Latin instructor used to say, "Just like English, only
different."

Latin is a very logical language, but the order of the
words is not a primary part of that logic. Children can
happily store away the information found in these books
without troubling themselves about what it all means.
They are not yet into the questioning, or dialectical,

stage. But you, the instructor, are well past that stage and may want to know what it all means. You can find information on various elementary Latin programs via the resource list at the back.

In the final analysis, learning the grammar of a language is not much good without learning the vocabulary. A good initial goal is to have two to three thousand words memorized within the first two years of study. This seems imposing but it works out to four words a day. This task is made even easier by the fact that many of the common Latin words have made their way into English. It should not be hard to learn the meaning of *frigidus*—cold. Or *femina*, which means woman, or *aqua*—water, and *poeta*—poet.

The Basics of Logic

Logic is concerned with evaluating arguments, and every academic subject involves arguments. Now, of course, in the sense intended here, we are not using the term "argument" to speak of some ugly quarrel between angry persons. In logic, an argument is a *reason* for believing something; an argument is an answer to a "Why?" question. As such, an argument has two important parts: a group of one or more premises and a conclusion. The premises are supposed to be like connected links in a chain from which the conclusion finally hangs. But not just any old connections between the links of the premises and conclusion will hang together properly. Argument links can either be good or bad. Logic is the discipline which shows us how to judge whether an argument is good or bad, whether it fits together properly or not.

We live in a culture which has been politicized and polarized. Consequently, we are tempted to respond favorably to the "applause lines" delivered by people who are on "our side," and to dismiss with contempt those who have said something with which we differ. We may often take sides in such a process, but it cannot be called *thinking*. People can say many true things couched in atrocious arguments, and they construct valid arguments in the cause of error.

As Christians, you want your children to come to the truth, but you must also want them to come through the door, and not as thieves and robbers. It is important to get to the conclusion the right way, as well as getting to the right conclusion. It is not enough to come up with the right answer—a blind squirrel can find a nut every once and a while.

One of the starting points in teaching logic is to enable the student to distinguish between the *structure* or the skeleton or basic framework of an argument and its *content*. The structure of an argument is like a railroad track; it guides the train, the content, along smooth lines. But the two things, the track and the train, are distinct, and each can have its own problems. We can also think of this difference between structure and content as comparable some common procedures in mathematics, especially algebra. In algebra, we can focus on the underlying structure of an equation by using variables that can stand for any numbers whatsoever. On the other hand, we can focus on the more concrete content of an equation by replacing the general variables with specific numbers. We find the same thing in logic, and so we need to get clear on how to evaluate both the structure and the content of an argument.

The primary concern when considering the structure of an argument is *validity*. Validity simply asks whether we have properly obeyed the general rules of argument structure, regardless of the content of the premises. If an argument shows we have not, then it is invalid; if it shows we have, then it is valid. To illustrate, suppose someone maintains that all dogs are Martians, and, that because Fido here is a dog, he must also be a Martian. This content is obviously not true, but the argumentation is valid, since it obeys a rule of logical inference. Validity means that the conclusion is necessarily true *if* the premises are *supposed as true for the sake of argument*. Validity simply seeks to ensure that we have stayed on the railroad tracks, regardless of the contents in the boxcars of our trains.

In a similar way, an invalid argument can be put together with true statements. Suppose someone maintains that Peter was an apostle, and that Abraham Lincoln was a President, and that, therefore, we may safely conclude that grass is green. We should have a problem with this. Everything about this is true except for the word *therefore*. The premises are true, and so is the conclusion, but the argument is poor. It is invalid; it jumps the railroad tracks. So granting that an opponent's argument is merely valid is no great compliment; crazy arguments can be valid. Having a valid argument, then, is only half the work. What we really want is an argument that is valid *and* has true premises—a *sound* argument. And soundness is a much more serious compliment than mere validity. Nonetheless, validity is crucial, and when we fail to make our arguments valid we are guilty of committing a *fallacy of form.*

One of the tools that is used in analyzing arguments is that of substituting symbols for prose. When a student learns how to do this, he is equipped to analyze the structure of an argument at a glance. Suppose someone said that (P) if it rains today, (Q) the farmers will leave the field. They then point out that (Q) the farmers did in fact leave the field, and conclude (P) that it must be raining. This is called the fallacy of affirming the consequent, which can be seen more readily when the argument is placed in symbolic form, where, in this case, capital letters are substituted for statements in the argument, as previously noted.

If P, then Q.
Q.
Therefore, P.

Any argument that takes this form is invalid—it does not matter what the statements behind the symbols are. In the same way, any argument which follows the form below is valid.

If P, then Q.
P.
Therefore, Q.

This form is called *modus ponens*, which is Latin for "way of affirming." It is valid regardless of the nouns put in the position of P and Q. If the structure follows this form, then the argument is valid. *Modus ponens* is just one example of a formal rule; there are many others. A good introductory logic textbook will take one through all the formal rules.

So, arguments may go awry by violating a formal rule, such as *modus ponens*, which focuses on the skeleton of an argument or by violating other standards, known as informal rules, which focus on the contents of the premises. Let's turn from briefly considering structure to consider problems in evaluating the contents of an argument.

We generally recognize three main types of *fallacies of content* or informal fallacies, namely, *relevance*, *inductive*, and *semantic* fallacies. Relevance fallacies are those arguments whose premise contents are irrelevant in supporting the conclusion, though they may appear relevant at first glance. Inductive fallacies are those arguments in which the likelihood of a conclusion is low or lower than intended. Semantic fallacies are arguments whose statements contain unclear terms which interfere with evaluating the argument.

One relevance fallacy is the *abusive ad hominem* fallacy in which one attempts to discredit a person's conclusion by discrediting their person. But someone can have a terrible character and yet have a wonderful argument; the two can be distinct. If the conclusion has nothing to do with the person's character, then discrediting their character is not relevant to the argument. Another fallacy of distraction was labeled by C.S. Lewis as *Bulverism*. This occurs when someone tries to answer an argument by simply explaining and pointing out the motive his opponent had in embracing the argument in the first place, *e.g.* "You are defending infant baptism simply because you admire the Puritans so much." Well, fine. But of course motives are entirely irrelevant to the validity or invalidity of any given argument. Other relevance fallacies include appeals to pity, popular sentiment, pseudoauthorities, etc. A good argument or counter-argument requires that the premises are truly relevant in supporting the conclusion.

One inductive fallacy is represented by another Latin phrase—*post hoc ergo propter hoc*. This means "after this, therefore because of this." It is the mistake of thinking that P caused Q just because P preceded Q in time. It is the mistake made by the man who thinks his shaving in the morning makes the sun rise. Other inductive fallacies include hasty generalizations, slippery slopes, and faulty analogies.

Finally, one semantic fallacy is *equivocation*, in which one shifts the meaning of an expression within an argument. For example, if someone claims that "it is right to allow everyone to take his or her own life, therefore, each of us has a right to his or her own body."

Here, the arguer equivocates on two different senses of the word "right," and the argument would fail. Other semantic fallacies include ambiguity, vagueness, and composition.

As mentioned above, the best time to teach logic is during the dialectic stage, which roughly corresponds to the junior-high years. Do not be misled; *average* twelve and thirteen-year olds are fully capable of mastering this material.

The Basics of Rhetoric

The word "rhetoric" has negative connotations for most people. It conjures up images of smooth politicians snowing their audiences with slick euphemisms and patriotic bombast as they attempt to remain in office with ever fatter salaries; of bellowing tyrants fanning huge crowds of mindless followers into a frenzy of genocidal xenophobia; of lugubriously ranting charlatans pacing stages with powerfully modulated semi-melodic syntactical sonorities; of wildly overblown descriptions like these.

That is an image of rhetoric that has plagued it for millennia. The first debate over rhetoric that we know of was between Plato and Aristotle: Plato said that public speakers—orators—were too concerned with style, with superficial flashiness in their words, with persuading audiences by means of fine-sounding eloquence instead of truth and substance. Aristotle agreed that skill in eloquence was often abused, but countered by asserting that the soundest logic is incommunicable without words and that therefore ability in rhetoric is necessary in order to be persuasive. The sophists of the Roman Empire were just that—merely sophists who charged audiences to listen to their highly entertaining speeches—because real political and legal debate was no longer crucial to the state: the emperor had taken over the functions of senate and supreme court. Eloquence got a bad name because of these circus rhetoricians. And yet Augustine argued that preachers should have skill with language in order to communicate spiritual truths to their audiences and to persuade them to obey that truth.

This debate has been repeated, with various changes rung on the same theme, ever since. But the attack is always made with great eloquence, as Plato's was, thus showing that rhetoric is unavoidable; and the answer is always essentially Aristotle's: communication through language is a characteristic of human beings and therefore we have only two choices—attempt to communicate and persuade by trial and error and accident, or think about what we are doing and try to refine, hone, and improve it.

In fact, Aristotle put rhetoric and logic in the same category. They are both arts of thought and communication that man does by nature, and that therefore must be refined. The rhetorician and the logician are not inventors of rhetoric and logic, any more than a grammarian is an inventor of grammar. They are all engaged in discovering what man does naturally and in cataloguing, categorizing, naming, critiquing, and communicating what they discover so that others may be more efficient in these naturally human arts.

The following basic principles of rhetoric, therefore, are to be considered in that light. They are principles developed in the Greco-Roman world and given renewed vigor in the Renaissance and Reformation; they are principles developed by observation of the way good speakers or writers work. They are not unbreakable rules, but they are steady guides until a student of persuasive communication understands, internalizes, and uses them well and is then able to manipulate ("break") them to his advantage.

Classical rhetoric divided itself into five "canons": (1) inventio, or the stage of developing arguments, illustrations, and substantive content; (2) dispositio, or the stage of arranging that accumulated content into the most advantageous order for persuasive communication; (3) elocutio, or the stage of considering how best to actually say all those things, what words and phrases to use, and what figures of speech; (4) memoria, or committing to memory the completed speech; and (5) pronuntiatio, or effective delivery of the speech. Most modern studies of rhetoric dispense with the last two as being concerned primarily with live oratory and concentrate on the first three as being applicable to a broad range of persuasive communication such as essay, speech, or letter writing, and formal speaking of all kinds.

In the first stage of developing a composition or speech ("inventio"), there are a number of considerations. What appeals will be effective: emotional, ethical, logical? Where logical arguments are used in a particular composition, what kind should they be: comparison/contrast, cause/effect, genus/species, definition? Where emotional appeals are used, how can the audience be moved without being manipulated? And how can the author/speaker impress the audience with his own integrity or credibility so that they will listen to him (the ethical appeal)?

In the "dispositio" stage, a typical order of the parts of a speech have been traditionally followed, though naturally with a great deal of variation. In this generic pattern, the first part, called "exordium," is the introduction. The second, "narratio," is the statement of the thesis or main point of the composition. The third part, called "divisio," outlines for the audience or reader the main divisions, headings, or points to be covered in the composition or speech. The fourth part, "confirmatio," is the actual argument or main discussion of the thesis under consideration; the fifth, "confutatio," is the refutation of possible objections; and sixth, the "conclusio," is the concluding statement, summary, or peroration. This traditional order admits of variation, adaptation, addition, elimination, and recombination of parts, but the essential principles are present in this scheme.

In the "elocutio" stage, the final stage of composition, the author chooses the level of style he will adopt (high, middle, plain), and considers his consistency of style, propriety of style for the occasion, and clarity of expression. He will also consider persuasive language devices such as figures of speech and word choice or diction.

It should be obvious by now that the fundamental principle behind all rhetorical study and practice is that the audience must be considered. Since we communicate not with ourselves but with others, communication involves an audience, whether it is the friend we write to, the congregation we preach to, or the readers we write for. And the audience implies a context and an occasion, both of which must also be taken into account in all the choices made in composition; and the audience either already has formed or will form an opinion of the author/speaker, and that too must be taken into account.

Behind all these principles lies a fundamental learning methodology that has far broader application than just the study of rhetoric. This method turns on the three stages called "art" (or precept), "imitation," and "practice." "Art" means learning the principles of a subject or study. "Imitation" means identifying and copying, in manner and style, and sometimes literally, the best models from the past. "Practice" means exercising oneself constantly in the attempt to incorporate all that has been learned from copying models into an original skill and style of one's own. When the student has diligently studied, copied, and practiced and has begun to internalize the habits of the art of rhetoric, he will discover that rhetoric is more than eloquence; it is a way of gathering, organizing, and using knowledge.

Paul says to the Corinthians that "my speech and my preaching were not with persuasive words of human wisdom, but in demonstration of the Spirit and of power" (1 Cor. 2:4), but clearly he uses words and uses them well. His objection is not to the skillful use of words, but to reliance on human persuasion and wisdom; but all gifts and abilities, including those of language, when submitted to the God who gave them become powerful tools for the edification of the saints, the dominion of the earth, and the advancement of the kingdom of God.

The Basics of Christian Worldview Thinking

We may conclude from a study of the greatest commandment that one of our central duties is to love God with all our *minds*. Moreover, in Deuteronomy 6:4-9, we are directed to impart the greatest commandment to our children when we get up, when we lie down, and when we walk along the road. In short, we are to be teaching our children this all-encompassing love for God, including an intellectual love for God, all the time.

In order to do this, we must first come to the recognition that God is over all, and in all, and through all. "For of Him and through Him and to Him are all things, to whom be glory forever. Amen" (Rom. 11:36). This recognition that God is sovereign over all things is central to the concept of thinking in a Christian fashion about anything. There is no neutrality in any area of human endeavor because of, and only because of, the sovereignty of God, and of His Son, the Lord Jesus Christ.

This conviction has been given many odious names down through history, but the most popular of such names is "Calvinism." It is important not to be put off by the prejudices generated by name-calling. (Remember the *abusive ad hominem* discussed above!) In order for Christian parents to understand and teach every subject in the light of the Lordship of Jesus Christ, they must first believe there *is* a relationship between Jesus Christ and the subject under consideration. And this is only possible when we understand that God is sovereign over all things.

The task of the Christian parent is to teach his children in such a way that all thoughts are brought under the headship of Christ. "For the weapons of our warfare are not carnal but mighty in God for pulling down strongholds, casting down arguments and every high thing that exalts itself against the knowledge of God, bringing every thought into captivity to the obedience of Christ" (2 Cor. 10:4-5).

We don't bring in this issue for the sake of being "divisive" or theologically cantankerous. It is simply a matter of historical record that the overwhelming number of Christians who have made contributions in the area of worldview thinking have been Christians who have acknowledged and embraced the doctrine of the sovereignty of God. We cannot readily yearn for the fruit but despise the tree it comes from. Given this, it is not surprising that we have so little fruit. Before we can make our way back, a little plain speaking is in order. Unless we recover the full-orbed theology of the Reformation, we will never recover the worldview thinking which is its child.

Fundamental to Christian worldview thinking is the biblical notion of *antithesis*. An antithesis is a sharp juxtaposition of two claims or views. Part of thinking like a Christian means that we aim to rid our outlook of all non-Christian assumptions about the world, history, human nature, knowledge, science, the arts, and every other subject. In its place we seek understanding from God's revelation on each and every concern, for in Christ "are hidden all the treasures of wisdom and knowledge" (Col. 2:3).

To be a Christian is to be in constant, total war. We have no say in the matter, and no one is exempt from serving. This war is not just some sideline feature of the Christian life. It *is* the Christian life. Every step toward seeing "every knee bow" before the Lord of glory is an act of war, whether in faithfulness or hatred. Until that point, the war is ruthless and relentless. The horrific enemy onslaught never ceases.

This war is not only constant but total, unconfined, and overwhelming. It is not limited to the daily fight against our own sin but encompasses everything within and without. It is not limited to our own or any one time but rages in every corner of history. It is not limited to our own flesh-and-blood world and history but is driven by dark clashes in heavenly places.

And as this battle moves us all along, killing and maiming, crushing and roaring, much of contemporary Christianity fights with bumper stickers and self-esteem seminars. As the enemy smiles and schemes to ravage our children and decapitate our churches, we try to play down our differences with our attackers and use their institutions as models for our own. As they mock Christ to His face, we learn to relax, take a joke, and create a more entertaining worship atmosphere. The only thing worse than being cut to death in the middle of a war is having it happen without realizing it.

How do God's people get to this point every so often? We do it by lust. Lust for our own supremacy. Lust for letting our own judgments be true, though God be made a liar. This unfaithfulness, after all, started the war. Our first parents enthroned themselves as judges over God, and we have inherited that family trait. God's enemies revel in the resulting rebellion, never ceasing to try to subvert the King, always denying the reality of the war.

After the initial rebellion, God *imposed* the war between His people and His enemies. It was no accident. The war was decreed. And so the battle has rampaged from Abel and Cain, Israel and Babylon, the apostolic fathers and the Gnostics, the Reformers and Rome to contemporary Christianity and modern egalitarianism.

Since this constant, total war is divinely imposed, we can hope for no peace except on the sovereign King's terms. To lust after peace and compromise in the midst of such a war is the highest form of rebellion. To seek peace and compromise when God calls for war is to seek to deface God Himself.

From Cain to the new intolerance, anti-Christian thinking has schemed to deny the reality of the total war. To admit it, of course, would be to admit sin. So, they must fabricate new fictions to whitewash over the division between the friends and enemies of God. They will insist that we are all one people, one planet, or part of god, not allowing any divisions at all. Or they try to shift the dividing line to that between classes, nations, or races. They will embrace anything as long as they can deny the divinely imposed war, and still fight against the people of God. As Augustine declared so long ago, "To the City of Man belong the enemies of God, . . . so inflamed with hatred against the City of God."

This attempted denial is so powerful and central to the enemy's agenda that they exert every effort to convince God's faithful to agree with them. As angels of light, they sucker the church into pagan attempts to save the earth, tolerate hatred of God, and tone down its "dogmatism" since everything is so fuzzy and unclear anyway. And the people that go whoring after such enticements will meet their just end: "I will return your retaliation upon your own head" (Joel 3:7).

How are we to do battle in this holy war? We ought to repent of our sinful failure to see the total war in its starkest Scriptural truth. We ought to pray for eyes to see through the wicked, yet innocent looking pretenses by which the enemy seeks to devour the Church, from fraudulent environmental values to idolatrous patriotism. *Christians ought to be the most skeptical and imaginative people on the face of the earth.* We ought, by God's Spirit, to discipline ourselves and our children in the Fruit of the Spirit, the testimony of faithful warfare. And, most assuredly, we ought to live in the unhesitating confidence that Christ has conquered the enemy, "having disarmed principalities and powers, He made a public spectacle of them, triumphing over them in it" (Col. 2:15).

What General Curriculum to Use

Classical education deals with students as individuals, and it is not bureaucratic in structure. The *desideratum* of such an education is not to produce a "cookie cutter" approach to learning. We don't seek to maintain quality control through some bureaucratic standard of measurement but rather through biblical *wisdom*. High standards in education are always *high*, but they are not always interchangeable, the way GM parts have to be. Two individuals may receive the same instruction, and yet, because of differences in gifts, personality, aptitude, and intelligence, the instruction may result in great differences in the students.

Coupled with all this is the fact that no one publisher "has it all." There is no package deal for classical and Christian education. This means that with many of the subjects you teach, it may be necessary to employ texts which are not "classical" in orientation. This is fine, because in the liberal arts, a tortured attachment to a particular textbook, as though it were the iron ball on the end of the chain, is itself an indication of a nonclassical approach to learning.

This means that your program will be eclectic. You will have to piece it together from various sources. As you do so, you shouldn't be frustrated that your curriculum is incomplete.

In preparation for this overall task, the reading you do should begin with the lists given at the back of this booklet. And we state emphatically, *again*, that the reading of the teacher is more important than the reading of the student. If the teacher reads as he should, the reading of the student will naturally fall into place. But if the teacher is just in search of a "book list" for the student to read, then it is not a classical and Christian education that is in view.

As the task of educating yourself and your children continues and broadens, you will always have a need for more books. And once your reading has begun in earnest, and you have gone down some of the bibliographic trails suggested by that reading, you will soon be in a position to start compiling your own book lists. Nevertheless, a few of our suggestions are listed below. Again, these are in addition to the books listed at the back of this booklet.

Without question, you will find much in the following reading which you should reject. The point is not to read all these authors with the idea of reconciling or harmonizing what they say. It cannot be done. But as thinking Christians, the fact that we are participating in the "great conversation," as Mortimer Adler put it, does not mean that we agree. As Christians we enter the conversation to present an apology for the Christian faith.

We should remember that with such preparatory reading, a good pace to maintain is to try and finish a book every week or two. This may seem intimidating at first, and if it were considered a hobby, it would be overwhelming. But the task is the education of your children, which is not a hobby but a *vocation*. The word *vocation* comes from the Latin verb *voco*, which means "I call." A person's vocation is his calling; a parent's vocation is to learn in order to teach.

Conclusion

Hopefully, this brief overview has supplied homeschool parents new to classical and Christian education a little more grounding in the subject. For those who start walking this sometimes arduous path, the long term blessings for you and your children and their children will far surpass the tangles along the way. So much is at stake. As the great nineteenth-century theologian, R.L. Dabney explained:

> The education of children for God is the most important business done on earth. It is the one business for which the earth exists. To it all politics, all war, all literature, all money-making, ought to be subordinated; and every parent especially ought to feel, every hour of the day, that, next to making his own calling and election sure, this is the end for which he is kept alive by God—this is his task on earth.[10]

Endnotes:

[1] Horace Bushnell, *Christian Nurture* (Cleveland: The Pilgrim Press, 1994, 1861), 36, 119.

[2] Cited in Richard Hofstadter,ed., *American Higher Education* Vol. 1 (Chicago: Univ. of Chicago Press, 1961), 17.

[3] Ibid., 54.

[4] Ibid., 39.

[5] Ibid., 8.

[6] Herbert Enderton, *A Mathematical Introduction to Logic* (New York: Academic Press, 1972) p.15.

[7] M. Bergman, et al, *The Logic Book* (New York: Ran dom House,1980) p. 6.

[8] R.M. Sainsbury, *Logical Form: An Introduction to Philosophical Logic* (Oxford: Blackwell, 1991), 8.

[9] Ibid., 30.

[10] R.L. Dabney, *On Secular Education*, ed. Douglas Wilson (Moscow: Canon Press, 1996), 3.

Beginning List of Readings in the Great Books

Ancient

The *Bible* should of course be read constantly.
Epic of Gilgamesh
The *Iliad* and *Odyssey* by Homer
The plays of Aeschylus, Sophocles, Euripides, and Aristophanes.
History by Herodotus
The History of the Peloponnesian War by Thucydides
The Lives of the Noble Grecians and Romans by Plutarch
Various dialogues of Plato
Nicomachean Ethics, Rhetoric, and *On Poetics* by Aristotle
On the Nature of Things by Lucretius
The *Annals* and *Histories* of Tacitus
The *Apocrypha*
The *Antiquities of the Jews* and *Wars of the Jews* by Josephus
The *Aeneid* by Virgil
Metamorphoses by Ovid
Meditations by Marcus Aurelius

Early Christian and Medieval

The *Didache*
Ecclesiastical History by Eusebius
On the Incarnation by Athanasius
Letter to the Corinthians by Clement
The *Koran*
Consolation of Philosophy by Boethius
Cur Deus Homo by Anselm
The Divine Comedy by Dante

Aquinas: Selected Writings (ed. Robert Goodwin)
The Prince by Machiavelli

Modern

Meditations on First Philosophy by Descartes
In Praise of Folly by Erasmus
The Bondage of the Will by Martin Luther
Commentary on Galatians by Martin Luther
Utopia by Thomas More
Hamlet, Macbeth, and *Much Ado About Nothing*
    by Shakespeare
Pilgrim's Progress by John Bunyan
Dialogues Concerning Natural Religion
    by David Hume
The Wealth of Nations by Adam Smith
Magnalia Christi Americana by Cotton Mather
Lectures in Sacred Rhetoric by R.L. Dabney
A Defense of Virginia and the South
    by R.L. Dabney
Pride and Prejudice by Jane Austen
The Foundations of Social Order by Rushdoony
Historical Theology by William Cunningham
The History of Christian Doctrine by Berkhof
Pilgrim's Regress by C.S. Lewis
The Twilight of Idols by Friedrich Nietzsche
Idols for Destruction by Schlossberg
Christianity and Liberalism by J. Gresham Machen
Postmodern Times by Edward Veith

Beginning List of Readings on Classical Topics

Education:

The Lost Tools of Learning by Dorothy Sayers
Recovering the Lost Tools of Learning
    by Douglas Wilson
*Repairing the Ruins: The Classical and Christian
    Challenge to Modern Education*
    ed. by D. Wilson
The Paideia of God and Other Essays on Education
    by Douglas Wilson
*The Well-Trained Mind: A Guide to Classical
    Education at Home* by Jessie Wise and
    Susan Wise Bauer
The Christian Philosophy of Education Explained
    by Stephen Perks
Logos Elementary and Secondary Curricula
    by Logos School, Moscow, Idaho
The Abolition of Man by C.S. Lewis
The Discarded Image by C.S. Lewis
An Experiment in Criticism by C.S. Lewis
The God Who is There by Francis Schaeffer
On Secular Education by R.L. Dabney
On Christian Doctrine/Book IV by Augustine
The Seven Laws of Teaching by John Milton Gregory

Literature and Reading:

*The Book Tree: A Christian Reference for Children's
    Literature* by Elizabeth McCallum
    and Jane Scott
*Invitation to the Classics: A Guide to What You've
    Always Wanted to Read* ed. by Os Guiness
*Heroes of the City of Man: A Christian Guide
    to Select Ancient Literature* by Peter Leithart

*The Brightest Heaven of Invention: A Christian
    Guide to Six Shakespeare Plays* by Peter Leithart
Ascent to Love: A Commentary on Dante's Comedy
    by Peter Leithart
How to Read a Book by Mortimer Adler
How to Read Slowly by James Sire

Logic:

Introductory Logic by Douglas Wilson
Intermediate Logic by James Nance
A Rulebook for Arguments by Anthony Weston
The Art of Reasoning with Symbolic Logic
    by David Kelley
Introduction to Logic by Leonard Copi
Logic by Gordon Clark
A Concise Logic by William Halverson

Rhetoric:

Rhetoric by Aristotle
Ad Herennium traditionally attributed to Cicero
Institutio Oratoria by Quintilian
Lectures in Sacred Rhetoric by R.L. Dabney
Classical Rhetoric for the Modern Student
    by Edward Corbett
Rhetoric in the Classical Tradition
    by Winifred Horner
Defense of Classical Rhetoric by Brian Vickers

Worldview Thinking:

The Bible
Through New Eyes by James Jordan
A House for My Name by Peter Leithart
*Plowing in Hope: Toward a Biblical Theology
    of Culture* by David Bruce Hegeman

Angels in the Architecture by Douglas Jones and
  Douglas Wilson
Institutes of the Christian Religion by John Calvin
Back to the Basics by Hagopian, Wilson, Jones,
  and Wagner
The City of God by Augustine
Mere Christianity by C.S. Lewis
The Defense of the Faith by Cornelius Van Til
Building a Christian Worldview
  by W. Andrew Hoffecker
Doctrine of the Knowledge of God by John Frame
War of the Worldviews by Gary DeMar

The following resources may be helpful in learning more about classical and Christian education. Some have different emphases and perspectives than others, but all can be helpful.

Canon Press
P.O. Box 8741
Moscow, ID 83843
800-488-2034
www.canonpress.org

Logos School Publications
110 Baker St.
Moscow, ID 83843
208-883-3199
www.logosschool.com

Veritas Press
1250 Belle Meade Dr.
Lancaster, PA 17601
800-922-5082
www.veritaspress.com

Greenleaf Press
1570 Old LaGuardo Rd.
Lebanon, TN 37087
615-449-1617
www.greenleafpress.com

American Classical League
Miami University
Oxford, OH 45056
513-529-7741
http://www.aclclassics.org

Association of Classical
and Christian Schools
www.accsedu.org

Schola Classical Tutorials
www.schola-tutorials.com

Escondido Tutorial Service
www.gbt.org

The Well-Trained Mind page
www.welltrainedmind.com

Classical Christian
Homeschooling
www.classicalhomeschooling.org

Classical Christian
Schooling Digest
ccsnet.org